T0315943

CARDIFF

THOSE WERE THE DAYS!

CARDIFF

THOSE WERE THE DAYS!

B R I A N   L E E

First published in Great Britain in 2003 by
The Breedon Books Publishing Company Limited
Breedon House, 3 The Parker Centre,
Derby, DE21 4SZ.

This paperback edition published in Great Britain in 2013 by DB
Publishing, an imprint of JMD Media Ltd

ISBN 978-1-78091-336-0

Printed and bound in the UK by Copytech (UK) Ltd Peterborough
.

CONTENTS

Author's
Acknowledgements

I would like to thank all those people who helped me in the compilation of this book. Special thanks go the editors of the *South Wales Echo*, *The Western Mail*, *The Post* and the *Cardiff Advertiser* for publishing my requests for photographs in their papers and, of course, to all those kind readers below who responded to my pleas. They are Peter Best, Alun Williams, Glyn Pockett MBE, Carl Allsopp, W.C. Fox, Christine Ashley, David Davies, Lorraine Barrett AM, John Smith, William Herbert, Gerry Lewis, Bill Rogers, Janet James, John Lyons, Christine Jones, Bill Rogers, Fred & Maureen MacCormack, Eveline Lewis, Valerie Beames, Sandra Chisnall, Brian O'Keefe, June Harvey, Max Pearce, Mary Brookes, June Taylor, Dulcie & Charles Vincent, Russell & Amanda Harvey, Donald Williams, Alan Margieson, Nicholas Yates, Mike Delgado, 'Slogger' Slocombe, Almera Evans, Jacqueline Lee, I. James, J. Jones, Ray Impney, B. Vizard, Les Gibbon, Clive Williams, John Billot, Glyn Potter, Alec McKinty, Neil Jones, Grace O' Donnell, Russell Waite, Marjorie Tanner, Janette Manson, Edith Edge, Lord Callaghan of Cardiff, Mr Perrins, Ted Williams, Kenneth Wakefield, Viv Sanson, Ivor Beaven, Mrs V.M. Davies-Thomas, Doug Lane, John Meazey, David Davies, FRIC of Stephenson & Alexander, The Capitol Centre Management team especially Centre Manager Jeff Wilson, Marketing and Promotions Manager Nia Williams and Administrator Sandra James, Ruth Hill, Graham J. Young, Roy Jefferies, headteacher of St Mary's School, Margaret Colley, Sheila Roberts, Matt Smith, Marketing Manager New Theatre, also Pam Ferguson and Chris Blackner. Finally, I ask forgiveness for any contributors who may feel they have been omitted from these acknowledgements and, as it has not been possible to trace copyright on some of the photographs, I apologise for any inadvertent infringement.

INTRODUCTION

IN 1989, I had the honour of writing the Foreword to Volume 21 of Stewart Williams's magnificent series of 36 *Cardiff Yesterday* books. It would be true to say that those books gave me the inspiration to branch out on my own, so to speak. That and the fact that in working as a stereotyper on *The Western Mail & Echo* for 28 years, when newspapers were printed in the old hot metal way, I developed a love for words and pictures or 'pix' as they say in the newspaper game.

Apart from the two years I spent doing my National Service, I have lived all my life in Cardiff and even on a fortnight's holiday abroad I get homesick after a week. During my 67 years, I have seen many changes to my beloved Cardiff and not all of them for the better. The filling in of the old Glamorgan Canal and the demolishing of the ruins of Herbert House in Greyfriars Road, the knocking down of the Empire Swimming Pool and the turning down of the proposal to build a racecourse at Pontcanna Fields in the 1950s are just some examples of acts of vandalism by our city fathers of the past.

Within the following pages, the reader will come across faces and places that in some instances will be familiar to him or her. Some of these images will, I am sure, bring a smile or two to those old enough to remember. Younger readers, I hope, when they take this stroll down Cardiff's memory lane, will be fascinated by the pictures of people and places that depict the Cardiff of yesterday.

The City of Cardiff is bidding for the European Capital of Culture 2008 UK Award and obviously I wish it well. After all it is, as the promotional press releases keep reminding us, 'A vibrant, cosmopolitan and forward looking capital with ambition'. This book, however, looks not to the future, but to the past and it is only by looking back that we can see where we are going.

Brian Lee
Cardiff
Summer 2003

A VANISHED CITY

Thirty years or so ago, many of the houses and buildings in the central area of the city were demolished, but the Golden Cross, right of picture, a listed building escaped the bulldozers.

Snelling House headquarters of the Welsh Gas Board can be seen right of picture.

When this photograph of Bute Terrace was taken in 1963, Snelling House was still being constructed.

St David Street. St David's Roman Catholic School right of picture is now just a memory.

The Hayes at the junction of Bridge Street and Mill Lane.

The open air fruit and vegetable market on the corner of Hayes Bridge Road and Mill Lane. The market moved to Bridge Street in 1981.

The New Moon Club in New Street occupied the top floor of the wholesale clothing warehouse which overlooked the market.

The Marriot Hotel now stands on the site of the open air market.

Bridge Street looking towards Hayes Bridge corner. The Queen's Head public house is right of picture.

The Queen's Head stood on the corner of Bridge Street and Union Street. Owens the gents hairdressers was on the opposite corner. Some Cardiffians will remember Happy Snaps the camera centre and Fry the second-hand bookshop also in the picture.

Huxley's Medical Stores was situated on the corner of Bridge Street and Barracks Lane.

All the houses in Union Street had been demolished when this picture was taken in the 1970s. The posters on both sides of the blocked up door of the Queen's Head, which closed in 1969, is advertising the pop group Hot Chocolate who were appearing at the Capitol Theatre.

Runwell the cyclists shop can clearly be seen in this picture of Mary Ann Street.

Bridge Street was quite a busy area when this picture was taken in the 1960s.

The popular John Bull Jaybe Stores which stood on the corner of The Hayes and Bridge Street.

Bridge Street looking towards Churchill Way.

Frederick Street. Larkins Warehouse is right of picture. The author, whose maternal grandparents lived at 59 Frederick Street, used to play on the steps of Larkins.

The Hayes was ready for redevelopment when this picture was taken in the 1960s.

The Lifeboat Tavern left of picture in Little Frederick Street was established around 1872. It stood less than 100 yards from the Dublin Arms and was demolished in 1978.

Little Frederick Street – looking towards Love Lane – before the bulldozers moved in.

The steeple of St David's Roman Catholic Cathedral in Charles Street can be seen left of picture. The white building in the centre is Seccombes which closed in 1977.

Hill Street looking towards David Morgan stores. Oxford House left of picture was under construction.

Union Street had seen better days when this picture was taken in the 1960s.

A deserted Millicent Street awaits demolition. One of the many city centre streets that were knocked down during the 1960s and 1970s.

The derelict building in the background is the Co-Operative Wholesale Society warehouse built in 1891.

The houses in the notorious Mary Ann Street had all been demolished when this picture was taken in the 1960s.

Houses in Tredegar Street and Mary Ann Street are razed to the ground. Something Hitler failed to do during World War Two.

There was not much left of Mary Ann Street when this picture was taken.

The inhabitants of these city dwellings were moved to council estates on the outskirts of the city. It is somewhat ironic that 50 years later luxury apartments are being built in the same area.

This is how the bottom end of Churchill Way looked in the 1960s.

The cars are parked where Barrack Lane and Union Street once stood. St David's Roman Catholic Cathedral is in the background.

The city centre had almost been completely demolished in the 1970s. The Pearl Assurance building, now known as Capital Tower, is shown in the centre of the picture.

The tall building on the left is Larkins and the building on the opposite side of the road is Brown Brothers Ltd.

This picture was taken from the rear window of 67 Bridge Street and shows Larkins in Frederick Street and Siemans and Brown Brothers Ltd in Hills Terrace.

There were plenty of car park spaces when Mary Ann Street was demolished. Snelling House can be seen in the background.

The once grand Cory Hall and YMCA buildings in Station Terrace were demolished in 1983. In 1901 David Lloyd George addressed a 'Peace Meeting' against the Boer War in the Cory Hall.

Amateur photographer Alun Williams took this picture of Guildford Crescent Swimming Baths in 1984, before it was demolished shortly afterwards.

Asteys Cellar Steak Bar on the corner of Park Lane and Queen Street had already been closed before the demolition of this area in 1982.

Calders the men's wear shop on the corner of Churchill Way and Queen Street before demolition. 1982.

Caroline Street had so many eating houses and pubs at one time that it was known as Grubb Street. It is thought to have been named after Queen Caroline who died in 1821 when the first residents of Caroline Street moved in.

Once the site of the open air market, the Marriot Hotel is now on the site. The King's Cross public house is to the right of picture.

The Cardiff Comrades Club and Institute in Paradise Place was demolished in 1987.

Cardiff docks: Once the premier port in the UK.

P. & A. Campbell
sailed their pleasure
steamers from the
Pierhead between
1886 and 1972.

View of the Channel Dry Dock.

Maltese Prince berthed in Queen Alexandra Dock, *c.*1948.

Demolition for these shops and houses in Bute Street was imminent when these pictures were taken in the 1960s. From the Canal Bridge on the Hayes, a long straight road leads down to the docks. Tram cars run swiftly up and down Bute Road, but the adventurer may prefer to walk down the most cosmopolitan thoroughfare in any city in Europe: J. Kyrle Fletcher, *Cardiff Notes: Picturesque and Biographical*, *c*.1902. These days, Bute Road is colloquially known as Bute Street.

The terraced houses in the Sophia Street area make way for the tall tower block flats in Loudoun Square.

The Bute Castle in Nelson Street had served its last pint when this picture was taken.

Bute Street Police Station, *c.*1967.

Diane Allsop (left) and her husband Raymond (right) from Butetown are seen in Loudoun Square Gardens, *c.*1950.

This area around Tredegar Street was in a run-down condition in 1981.

AROUND AND ABOUT

The turn of the century and a rare view of Cardiff Castle and the houses then in front of it.

Aerial view of Cardiff Castle. The famous Cardiff Arms Park is bottom left of the picture.

This was how Cardiff Arms Park looked in the 1930s. The terraced houses in the forefront of the picture were in an area once known as Temperance Town.

Pengam Airport opened in 1930. By 1938 a regular hourly service flight to Weston-Super-Mare was in operation. The airport was used by the RAF during the war as a maintenance centre, 1951.

The Job Centre now rests on the corner of Charles Street and Bridge Street.

Charles Street was named after Charles Vachell, a mayor of Cardiff. St David's Roman Catholic Cathedral can be seen in the distance.

The Globe on the corner of Castle Street and Womanby Street. A sirloin steak in the upstairs Astral Bar and Grill cost eight shillings (40p).

Whitbread and Co. Ltd. Warehouse and distribution centre stood on the corner of Penarth Road and Taffs Mead Embankment. It opened as a bottling store in 1932 and closed in 1963. The company supplied the ocean liners *Queen Mary* and *Queen Elizabeth*.

Southgate House was built on the site of the Wood Street Congregational Church (top picture opposite page). Four workers were sadly killed in 1978 when a construction cable fell 100 feet.

The Wood Street Congregational Church was demolished in 1972. It was once the Temperance Town Music Hall.

St Dyfrig's Church, Wood Street, was demolished in 1979.

The City Planning offices later stood on the site of St Dyfrig's Church in the previous picture.

Highfields Inn, Ely, was once a farmhouse.

Another well-known Ely 'watering hole' was the Dusty Forge established around 1790. It is now a thriving youth centre.

The White Lion was a popular pub with the Ely Paper Mills workers.

Ely Bridge dates back to Roman times and was rebuilt in 1969 at a cost of £75,000.

In 1960, the Canton area of the city was flooded and not for the first time either!

Highcroft, Newport Road, *c.*1950. A police station was later built near the site.

A flooded Cowbridge Road East, 1960.

Children playing around a maintenance barge loaded with grass cuttings, Llandaff north, c.1940.

A truly idyllic scene! These youngsters are fishing in the Glamorgan Canal at the Gabalfa lock, *c*.1940.

Workers at the Mellingriffith tin plate works at Whitchurch lived in these houses which were known as Sunnybank Cottages. Only the wall in front of them remains.

The lock at Mynachdy. The last barge passed down the Glamorgan Canal in 1942 and the canal was later sadly filled in.

FAMOUS FACES

Prince William waves to the crowd. His first official engagement at the launch of the Cardiff Marketing Board. Also in the picture are his mother the Princess of Wales, The Lord Mayor John Smith and the Lord Lieutenant of Glamorgan, Captain Norman Lloyd-Edwards. 1 March 1991.

The Princess of Wales on another visit is being introduced to the Lady Mayoress Ellen Herbert by her husband, the Lord Mayor Bill Herbert, 1988.

The Prince of Wales chatting to Chief Officer Les Claxton on a visit to Cardiff Prison in 1979. John McCarthy, the Prison Governor, is pictured first left.

Princess Anne is greeted by the Lord Mayor Bill Herbert on her visit to Cardiff Prison in 1988.

Pope John Paul on his papal visit to Cardiff, 1982.

Archbishop Runcie M.M. of Canterbury, signing the visitors book in the Lord Mayor's parlour. Also in the picture, Lord Mayor John Smith and Lady Mayoress Monica Walsh, August 1991.

Making a presentation to international singing star Tony Bennett at the Capitol Theatre is Bill Rogers, General Manager of Littlewoods, and staff member Lyn Pearson, 1973.

Mrs Nell Dickinson, of Cardiff, looking through a brochure for her holiday for two, a six-day tour of Switzerland, presented by Hourmont Travel. Left to right: Bill Rogers, general manager of Littlewoods, Welsh singer Ivor Emmanuel, Bob Hourmont, and comedian Jack Douglas, c.1970.

Lord Mayor Bill Herbert holding up a Gren cartoon on the occasion of Viscount Tonypandy George Thomas's 80th birthday celebrations at the City Hall, 1988.

Viscount Tonypandy George Thomas signing the visitors book in the Lord Mayor's parlour. Also in the picture are Lady Mayoress Monica Walsh, Lord Mayor John Smith, Chairman Bill Bowen and the High Sheriff of Glamorgan Mr B.K. Thomas, 1990.

Wales's much loved Harry Secombe (centre) shares a joke with New Theatre administrator Peter Lea and his wife Linda.

Mr & Mrs D. Matt from Barry were the first £500 prize winners in the New Theatre's lottery. They are seen receiving their cheque from band leader Victor Silvester Jnr.

The Variety Club of Great Britain presented the New Theatre with a plaque in appreciation of the theatre's continuing support. Welsh comedian Wyn Calvin is shown presenting the plaque to Peter Lea, Administrator of the New Theatre, 1976

Female impersonator Danny Le Rue with Wyn Calvin and comedian Dickie Henderson.

The Lord Mayor Phil Dunleavy and his guests posed for this picture in the Lord Mayor's parlour. Far right is Victor Spinetti who starred with fellow Welshman Richard Burton in the film *The Taming of the Shrew*, c.1982.

Australian-born actor John McCallum (centre) is sitting next to his wife Googie Withers (right). They were both appearing in a play at the New Theatre.

Jack Douglas presenting Ruth Madoc and her husband John Jackson with a wedding anniversary cake. Norman Vaughan and the rest of the cast are all smiles.

Comedian Jimmy Tarbuck, Pat Flaven and the Lord and Lady Mayoress at a charity function in the City Hall.

Welsh actress Rachel Thomas signing the visitors book in the City Hall. She left her Cardiff classroom to star with Paul Robeson in *The Proud Valley*.

Another well-known Welsh actor who signed the visitors book was Philip Madoc (Ruth Madoc's first husband) who has been dubbed 'British Television's all-purpose foreigner'.

Falklands War hero Simon Weston signing the visitors book in the Lord Mayor's parlour, 1990.

Cardiff-born athlete Colin Jackson, world record holder for the 110 metres hurdles event and Britain's most 'capped' athlete, swops 'medals' with the Lord Mayor Bill Herbert, 1988.

Norman Wisdom, who was appearing in his one-man show at St David's Hall, invited Mrs Amanda Harvey and her son James to meet him backstage and kindly posed with them for this picture in 1995.

Keith Harris and Orville who appeared in the pantomime *Humpty Dumpty* at the New Theatre in 1984.

HAPPIEST DAYS OF THEIR LIVES

Pupils of St Mary's Roman Catholic School, Canton. The teacher is Tom Kiely, *c.*1940.

Chemistry class, St Mary's Roman Catholic School, *c.*1940.

Woodwork class, St Mary's Roman Catholic School. Class teacher Mr Doran can be seen in the background, c.1940.

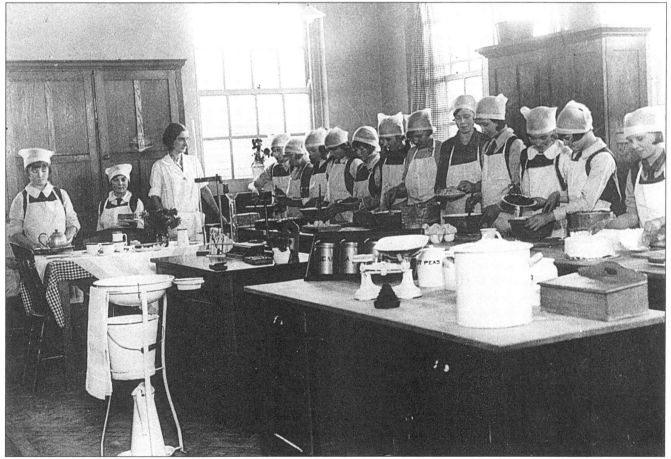

Miss Dillon's cookery class, St Mary's Roman Catholic School, c.1940.

These St Mary's Roman Catholic School young ladies appear to be having a handicraft lesson, *c*.1940.

Herbert Thompson Infants School, Ely, *c*.1939.

St Peter's Roman Catholic School, infants class, *c.*1938.

St Peter's Roman Catholic School, infants class, *c.*1943. The girl with the big ribbon in her hair, fourth from the left front row, is Valerie Beames née Lee.

Tredegarville School, infants class, *c.*1943.

St Cuthbert's School, standard 1-2, *c.*1945.

King's College class of 1948.

Our Lady's Convent
pilgrimage to Lourdes. In
the background is Sister
Mary Wilfridge, 1954.

These St David's Junior School pupils were dressed as sailors for St David's Day. Left to right: Roy Jones, Brian O'Keefe, Dennis Flannagan, Eugine Pasticio, Tommy Walsh, Anthony Harris and Philip Male, c.1950.

<#>

In 1955 the pupils of Gladstone School performed Bernard Shaw's play *St Joan*. June Thomas wearing white played the lead.

Gladstone School's 1955 production of Shakespeare's *Midsummer Night's Dream.*

Gladstone School concert. Some of the young ladies who took part were Marie Cork, Sally Jackson, Iris East, June Rees, Jill McClennan, Valerie Nevard, and Ann Bellringer, *c.*1954.

St David's Day celebrations at Cae Glas Junior School, Rumney, 1958.

Members of Kingsway Hall Mission, Harriet Street, Cathays. Extreme left seated is Eveline Nicholls. Barbara Statton and Avril Hodges are in the back row third and fourth respectively from the left, *c.*1952.

Pupils of St Joseph's Convent School, North Road. Second right in the back row is Joan O'Callaghan who, in later life, found fame as film star Anna Kashfi. She married Marlon Brando in 1957 and starred with film legends Spencer Tracy, Robert Wagner and Rock Hudson.

Windsor Clive Junior School. These pretty young ladies won the Cardiff Schools and the Ely Schools relays cups. Left to right standing: Pauline Marsh, Sylvia Simpson, Valerie Clements. Seated: Marlene (surname unknown), Pamela Arrowsmith, June Williams, 1951.

Gladstone School netball team, *c*.1955.

Fairwater Infants School, *c.*1969.

Llanedeyrn High School rugby team, 1974–5.

1st Company Cardiff Boys Brigade, Fairwater Presbyterian Church staged a *Snow White and the Seven Dwarfs* pantomime, Spotlight, 1973.

<#>

Cae Glas Junior School football team. Seated top left back row is Steve Derret who went on to play for Cardiff City and Wales. Others in the picture include Phil Chamberlain, Harvey Coles and Max Pearce.

Eleanor Street School winners of the Seager Cup, 1948–9.

Gladstone School house captains. Left to right: R. Sneddon, A. Boul, A. Williams, K. Sutton, 1947.

Gladstone School baseball team, 1947.

Llanrumney High School, form two, 1972.

St Patrick's football team, Schools Division Two champions, 1955–6. Back row (left to right): D. Pool, D. McNamara, J. Swaine, A. Conway, J. O'Brien, G. Lewis. Front row: B. Whelan, G. Howells, M. Sullivan, L. Patterson, B. Lewis.

Getting ready for parade are, left to right, Don Williams, Seymour Gould and Ted Williams. They were members of the 2nd Company Boys' Brigade at Clare Gardens Methodist Church, Riverside, in late 1943. The marching and drilling gave a good grounding for the compulsory National Service in the armed forces to follow.

2nd Company Boys' Life Brigade team. In the background are Mr W.G. Phillips, leader in charge, and his assistant. A carpenter by trade, Mr Phillips held classes for the boys which gave them good experience for their future. Among the boys are Don Williams, Raymond Bennet, Gerald Cummins and Fred Lewis.

The senior boys of Kitchener Road School visited the Cromlech at Wenvoe and obviously the health and safety rules were not stringently applied in 1944.

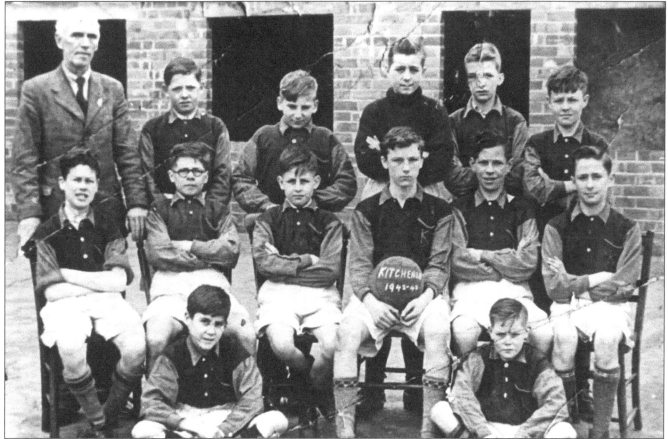

Kitchener Road School football team, 1943. Left of the back row is Mr Thomas (Bsc), a well-liked teacher who was always proud of his boys' achievements. The player with the ball is the captain, John Baldock.

Howard Gardens High School 1st XI cricket team, 1946. Back row (left to right): Mr D. Williams, K. Herniman, P. Cragg, O. Wilson, D. Ash, H.B. Jones, Mr J.D. Byrd. Front: D.P. Honey, M. Cuming, J. Baker, A. Margerison (captain), N. Williams, G. Probert, F. Shachell.

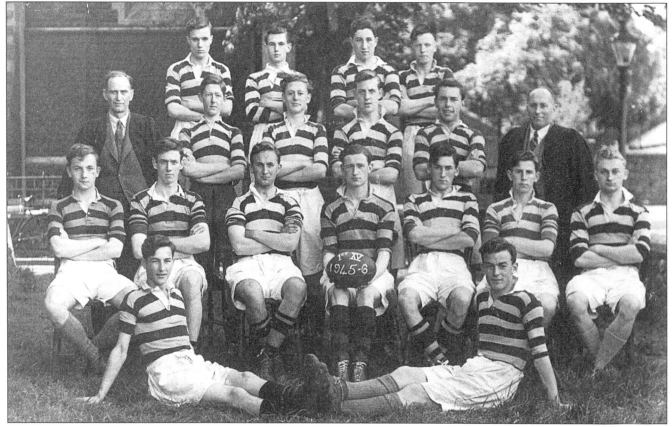

Howard Gardens High School 1st XV rugby team, 1945–6.

Howard Gardens High School athletics team, 13 June 1947.

Howard Gardens High School 1st XV rugby team 1944–5.

Waterhall School, Fairwater, under-15s rugby team, 1966–7.

Lady Mary Roman Catholic School soccer team, 1971–2.

Lady Mary Roman Catholic School rugby team, 1971–2.

St Mary's Roman Catholic School rugby team, 1971–2.

St Mary's Roman Catholic School baseball team, c.1971.

St Mary's Roman Catholic School 1st XV, 1956–7. Back row (left to right): Terry Williams, Dennis O'Driscoll, Danny McDonnell, Mr T. McCabe (headmaster), Tony Hurford, John Cason, Alan Venables, Michael Donovan, Mr T. Sullivan (sports master), Bernard Miller, Willie O'Donough. Front: Ron Mickelson, Liam Latchford, Danny Stone, Bill Brookman, Michael Murphy, David Hole, Terry O'Gorman.

22nd Cardiff Boys' Brigade (Rumney Methodist) under-12s soccer team in May 1994. Back row (left to right): Mark Atkins, Matthew Ball, David Ball, Michael Sully, Nathaniel Grace, Paul Whitcombe, James Harvey. Front: Neil McDonald, Dean Hobbs, Martin Taylor, Mark Partridge, Matthew Davies, Stephen Brookes. The team dropped only one point all season, scoring 59 goals and conceding only 11.

Pictured after having a 'kickaround' in 1969 are back row (left to right): Amin Mahamed, Andrew Stickler, Mark Canter, James O'Brien, Michael Day. Front: Anthony Delvalle, Terry Stickler, Nicholas Yates, Shaun Stickler, Andrew Day, John Fitzpatrick, Mark McCormack.

Peter Lea School baseball team, *c.*1958. Back row (left to right): K. Morris, P. Bishop, J. Howells. Middle: P. Snook, B. Harding, S. Morgan, R. Delgado, W. Payne, R. Parslow. Front: Mr B. Harry, D. Webber, M. Gorey, W. Davey (captain), G. Eveleigh, T. Proctor, Mr S. Hocking.

Waterhall School, form one, *c.*1959.

Waterhall School, Conway House class, *c.*1960.

Whitchurch High School, 6th form, 1990.

Gladstone School Juniors cricket team, 1978–9. The teacher on the left is the well-known local historian, Bill Barrett.

Whitchurch Junior Judo Club, March 1999.

LEISURE AND PLEASURE

The New Theatre, built in 1906, has offered the public a large range of entertainment from pantomime to ballet.

The much loved Plaza cinema in Gabalfa opened on 12 March 1928 and closed on 17 October 1981 and has been replaced by a retirement housing complex.

Western Mail & Echo staff dance at Bindles, Barry. Left to right: Jacqueline Lee, Brian Lee, John Sweeney, Ann Sweeney, David Jones, Francis Jones, Valerie Beames, Malcolm Beames, Bert Oakey, Liz Oakey, *c*.1966.

Western Mail & Echo staff dance, Bindles, Barry, *c*.1955.

Cardiff City Police Ball, City Hall, 1955.

Welsh singer Ivor Emmanuel was the centre of attraction at the Cardiff City Police dance at the Connaught Rooms, *c.*1955.

Girls from the Alma School of Dancing are put through their paces, *c.*1973.

Cinderella pantomime, St Peter's Theatre group, January 1956.

Cardiff boilermakers getting in the mood before setting out for the 1950 Ireland v Wales rugby international. First left is Bill Lewis. Others in the picture include Pat Sexton, Joe Pattern and Harry Cashman. For the record, Wales won by two tries (six points) to one penalty goal (three points).

Sir Percy Thomas (of Percy Thomas & Son, architects) receiving a Christmas gift from his staff at the office Christmas party at the Royal Hotel, 1955.

These Cardiff Prison officers went on a charity walk in the Brecon Beacons, *c.*1980.

Musical conductor Edward G. Charles, affectionately known as 'The Music Man'. In 1947 he formed the Cardiff Juvenile Temperance Festival Choir which consisted of 150 young girls and a few boys. The choir travelled to many parts of the world, including Germany, USA and France.

Members of Cyncoed Methodist Church Choir, Griffin Inn in July 1979. Left to right: Geoff Trinnick, Joe Ambridge, Mrs Bradburn, Mrs Alethea Evans and Mrs Davies.

These policemen appear to be guarding the boxing belts of Jack Petersen, Dai Dower and Joe Erskine at a City Hall charity ball.

The Legion Extras skittles team from the British Legion at Whitchurch, were winners of the Champion of Champions Skittles Cup, c.1968. Bill Ford is seen holding the trophy as well as a pint in his other hand!

Cathays Conservative Club outing, 1948.

Cathays Conservative Club outing, 1952.

The Cardiff Star Jazz Band's Bedford Super Vega Duple bus, *c.*1970.

The Cardiff Star Jazz Band, *c.*1981.

Wayne Vincent, who played the part of Fagan in Cantonian High School's production of *Oliver* in 1980, getting made up for the part.

The eight regional darts winners who played for the News Of The World Welsh title at the City Hall, 1955.

A celebration dinner was held for Len Baker who won the News Of The World darts Welsh title in 1960.

Winners of the Welsh and British Isles Rinks Championship in 1965 were these members of Rhiwbina Bowls Club. Left to right: Rundle Bending, W.D. Jones, Jock Thomson and Towyn Roberts.

Winners of the Montaque Burton Table Tennis Cup in 1956 were Roath Road's 'C' team. Standing (left to right): Peter Doughty, Bobby Miller. Seated: Doug Etton, Jeff Jones and Jim Davies. The Roath Road club played in Fanny Street Lane at the rear of the Chapman's Removal building.

A raft race took place in 1968 from Cardiff to Taffs Well. This team from the Newport College of Technology obviously got into trouble crossing Llandaff Weir.

Members of the Cardiff Writers' Circle on a visit to the offices of the *Western Mail & Echo* in 1967.

One of the *Spotlight* shows staged by the 1st Company Cardiff Boys' Brigade. Andrew Rendell, Stephen Dover, Steve Williams, Peter Hamer and Nicholas Vincent were some of the actors who took part, *c.*1970.

Members of the Municipal Club, City Road, enjoying themselves at a sports presentation evening in 1960.

Bethany Baptist formed this Brownie pack when they moved to their new location in Rhiwbina. This picture shows Brown Owl, Mrs Eileen Thomas (centre) flanked by Mrs Pat Elkington (left) and Kay Kemp (right), 1967.

These children from the Oak House, Hollybush estate, Whitchurch, posed for this photograph at their Christmas party in 1965.

SPECIAL OCCASIONS

In 1968 Welsh soccer hero John Charles 'The Gentle Giant' (extreme left) was best man at the wedding of Cardiff sportsman Glyn Potter and Ann Morgan. Stefan Terlezki, who became MP for Cardiff West in 1983, looks on.

A presentation to Jim Brimmel, Britain's top boxing referee, took place at the Royal Hotel, Cardiff. Left to right: Dai Corp, Howard Winstone, Brian Rennie, Jim Brimmel, Jack Petersen, Eddie Thomas and Glyn Potter, c.1970.

Phil Bennett, who during his international rugby career set numerous scoring records when playing for Wales and the British Lions, was presented with a miner's lamp at the Star Leisure Centre, Splott, c.1974.

Community Police Constable Graham Hill visited Gladstone School and is seen here with some of the pupils, 1981.

Lord Mayor Bill Herbert (fourth from left) with members of the Cardiff City Social Club at a charity function in the Lord Mayor's Mansion, *c*.1988.

Sir Julian Hodge (centre) is flanked by the Lord Mayor and Lady Mayoress at the opening of the Julian Hodge Bank, 1988.

All the hustle and bustle in Crwys Hall Presbyterian Church, Monthermer Road, Cathays, when members undertook a complete renovation project back in 1965. Sadly, however, the congregation dwindled and the church was closed in 1996. It was later purchased by an evangelical group and is now known as Highfields.

A thanksgiving service was held in Crwys Hall Presbyterian Church in 1965 after members had themselves carried out a complete renovation.

Lord Mayor John Smith at 'The Blessing of the Waters' service. Greek Orthodox Community, Epiphany holy day, East Dock, January 1992.

The top picture shows singer Mary O'Hara with New Theatre administrator Peter Lea drawing the winning ticket for the first prize in the New Theatre's October lottery. And in the bottom picture opera singer Clair Powell does the honours, c.1970.

St David's Day concert at Fairwater School in 1965. Two of the drummer boys are Howard Poland (wearing a leek) and Nicholas Vincent (wearing a daffodil) who stills plays the drums today!

<#>

Welsh rugby international Bleddyn Williams, boxers Joe Erskine and Dick Richardson and Welsh soccer international Trevor Ford were just some of the sports personalities who attended the Victoria Ballroom, Canton, in 1955 for a fund raising evening in aid of the widow of former England 'B' centre-half Leon Leuty. Leuty and Chick Musson, his Derby County colleague from the 1946 FA Cup-winning team, died within weeks of each other, both only in their mid-30s.

The inauguration of the Lord Mayor John Smith at the City Hall. Charles Ackerman, Sergeant at Arms (left), and Bill Surringer, mace bearer (right), 1991.

The Lord Mayor John Smith being sworn in by councillor Bill Herbert, 1991.

Brian Lee, co-ordinator of the City Hall-based Historic Records Project, introduces project photographer Lee Thompson to the Lord Mayor, Bill Herbert, at the launch of the project's 'A Cardiff Notebook', 1988.

In 1991, Miss World was a visitor to the Lord Mayor's parlour. With the Lord Mayor and Lady Mayoress are Mr and Mrs Lyn Jones of the Variety Club.

Harry Polloway, the well-known toast master, with Molly Moon and swordbearer Sam Smith at the Mayoral Installation, City Hall, 1990.

Workers of the World Unite! An unemployment march was held in the city centre, June 1981.

Regulars of the Fox and Hounds, Whitchurch, on a day trip to Worcester Races stopped on their way to pose for this picture, c.1955.

Scout group from St Paul's Church, Grangetown, *c.*1933.

For these docklands children, 7 April 1953 was a special day. The driver of this car disappeared soon after he crashed the car into the Pierhead railings. He was later traced.

James Callaghan, the Labour MP for Cardiff South-East and Penarth, is seen here with two of his constituents. He became Prime Minister in 1976.

The staff of the Mellingriffith Works visited the City Hall in June 1934. The gentleman in the first row (centre) is Hubert Spence Thomas, owner of the works. In the back row (extreme left) is Tom Gibbon, a foreman at the works.

On the 20 March 1966, members of the National Trollybus Association went on the last trolleybus trip to the Pierhead.

The Wild West was the theme for St Augustine's Church Fayre, Rumney, 1999. Standing (left to right) are Margaret Birchall, Amanda Harvey, Marilyn Collard. Kneeling: Revd Canon David Hathaway and Margaret Taylor.

CELEBRATIONS!

St Patrick's Pipe Band marching through Pentrebane Street, Grangetown. The drum major Des Walsh was a well-known baseball player, *c.*1961.

Canon Thomas Phelan of St Patrick's Church blessing the pipe band, *c.*1961.

St Patrick's Pipe Band posed for this picture in Grangetown Gardens, c.1961.

The young girl wearing the crown is Valerie Cousins, Adamsdown Carnival Queen of 1946. The long haired girl alongside her is Thelma Burston. Others in the picture are Marjorie Jones, Marjorie Emmett, Nancy Poole, Jean Gallivan and Freddie Jones.

Jim Callaghan, now Lord Callaghan of Cardiff, with the Adamsdown May Queen of 1947, believed to be Marie George. Her attendants were Ann Jones, Renee Todd, Joyce Gallivan and Ann Duffield.

Jim Callaghan judging the fancy dress competition, Adamsdown May Day Carnival, 1947.

Some of the fancy dress competitors at the Adamsdown May Day Carnival, 1947.

Post-war celebrations in Whitchurch. A fancy dress competition was held and Mr and Mrs John Bull were Gerry Monte and Jeanette Manson.

Whitchurch Rugby Club Easter fancy dress walk, 1968.

Children from Fitzroy Street and Wyeverne Road, Cathays, took part in a fancy dress competition to celebrate the end of World War Two. Ruth Jones as Miss Peace won first prize.

Residents of Gwennyth Street, Cathays, VE Day Party, 1945.

VE Day celebrations in Little Wyeverne Road, Cathays, 1945.

Residents of Bedford Street, Roath, seem to be enjoying themselves at this street party on the occasion of the Queen's Coronation, 2 June 1953.

Dalton Street, Cathays, celebrated the Queen's Coronation with a fancy dress competition.

In Severn Road, Canton, the residents held a parade for the 1953 Coronation. Wearing a nightcap and shawl towards the rear is Mrs Hetty Carpenter.

Tina Hill from Wyeverne Road, May Queen of Cathays, adjusting her headgear,1 May 1981.

The residents of Whitchurch celebrating the wedding of the Prince and Princess of Wales, July 1981.

Michelle King, Vincent Hill and Lorna Smith of the Cathays Bingo Club in celebratory mood on the occasion of the Duke and Duchess of York's marriage.

The night they invented champagne! Marilyn King, Michelle King, Tina Hall, Ruth Hall, Lorna Smith and Carol Smith get ready to make a toast.

Miss Susan Dennis, the New Theatre's 10,000th member, is presented with a magnum of champagne by chairman Jack Tiffin. Looking on are secretary Arthur Morris Jones (left) and treasurer Colin Tucker.

South Wales Echo editor Geoff Rich presents Alun Williams, of Rhiwbina (left), with 100 gallons of free petrol vouchers. He won first prize in the *Echo's* Motoring Festival competition, 1980.

These Cardiff schoolboys attended a Duke of Edinburgh's Award reception at Buckingham Palace for all those pupils who attained the gold medal standard. Back row (left to right): Ian Berridge, Andrew Murray, Stephen Carter, Michael Doolan, Andrew Rendle and Nick Vincent. Front: Lawrence Aquilner, Keith Stevens, Billy Thomas, Stephen Ashman, Kerry Rhoden and Howard Crabbe.

The staff of Cardiff Prison have their photograph taken in front of the prison's Christmas tree, c.1980.

Prison officers held a senior citizens' Christmas party in Cardiff Prison. The carol singers are Les Parry, Steve Davies, Norman Bass, Eric Baker, Janet Williams, Jimmy Werritt and Mike Griffiths, *c*.1985.

The Lord Mayor, J.C. Edwards, presents a cheque and a certificate to Cathays Community Centre in 1980. Left to right: Constable Graham Hill, Pam Waddle, Celia McConkey and the manager of the centre.

The Lord Mayor, John Smith, and Lady Mayoress, Monica Walsh, attended the centenary celebrations of the Central Market in 1991.

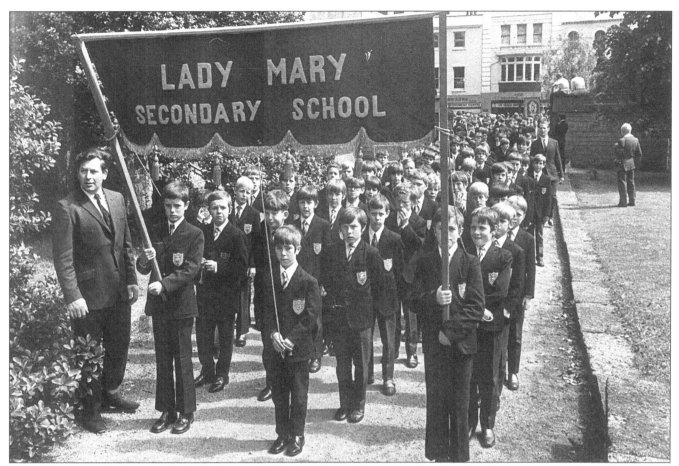

Pupils of Lady Mary Roman Catholic School with teacher Frank Callus at Corpus Christi celebrations, *c.*1970.

The pupils of St Mary's Roman Catholic School line up outside Asteys in Wood Street in preparation for the Corpus Christi procession.

St Joseph's Roman Catholic School girls at the Corpus Christi celebrations, Cardiff Castle grounds, *c.*1970.

Pictured outside St David's Roman Catholic Cathedral at the Lord Mayor's inauguration service are Sir James Lyon, Councillor Bill Bowen, Gwilyn Jones MP and Roger Paine, chief executive Cardiff City Council, June 1990.

Pupils of St Mary's Roman Catholic School sat for this photograph in the school playground before joining in the Corpus Christi celebrations.

WORLD OF WORK

The Tudor Graphic print works was established in the 1800s. It later became home to the commercial operations of the *Western Mail & Echo*. Qualitex bought the business in 1966. Keyboard operator Percy Bishop (fifth right seated) can be seen with a silver salver plate he was presented with for 50 years service to the company, May 1967.

The old Tudor Graphic composing room, *c.*1950.

In the top picture, the compositors have obviously posed for the photographer.

In this one they seem hard at work, *c.*1966.

Gordon Poole operating the Wohlenberg Guillotine Machine, Qualitex Printing Works, *c.*1966.

All hands to the deck! The Qualitex binding room is a hive of activity, *c.*1966.

Eddie Denty operating the litho plate machine. Qualitex, *c.*1966.

Maurice Nolan positioning plates on the registration machine. Qualitex, *c.*1966.

Artists at work in Qualitex's art studios, *c.*1966.

The Qualitex pre-press typesetting room was situated in the old casting room. Left to right: D. Simpkins, D. Deans, D. Major, P. Sweetman, D. Clements and A. Williams, 1987.

Monotype Keyboard Department, Qualitex. The man at the desk is Alun Williams. Others in the picture are Ron Watson, John Pearce, Ray Lewis, Percy Bishop, Mike Manley and Roy Hancock, *c.*1966.

Hard at work on the keyboards in this picture are Mike Manley, Ron Watson, Alun Williams, George Lewis and Percy Bishop, c.1963.

This was how Qualitex's machine room looked in the 1960s.

Tudor Graphic's management team.

Seems hard to believe that these employees of Meggitt & Jones, timber importers, posed for this picture more than half-a-century ago back in 1952.

Mr Fred Robinson, of Tweedsmuir Road, Tremorfa, is pictured being presented with a long service cheque by director Mr Gareth Hughes in 1975. Mr Robinson joined Meggitt & Price, Barry Timber Importers, straight from school in 1925 and worked as a tallyman at the timber yard.

Clerical staff who worked for Spillers Flour Mills at Roath Dock in 1956.

Office staff, Marments Ltd, June 1958.

Mr Prescott receiving a 'workmate bench' retirement present from Mr Terry Cleary, transport manager, British Iron & Steel Works, East Moor Road, *c.*1970.

British Iron & Steel Works traffic manager Frank Ackerman presenting a retirement cheque to Mr Dean, *c.*1970.

Cardiff Prison officers Clive Willetts, Mike Griffiths and John Morley, *c.*1980.

Cardiff Prison officer Ron Shellard presents fellow officer Mike Griffiths with a cheque for a £1,000 his winnings in the Cardiff City FC lottery.

Cardiff GPO apprentice course, Penarth. The young man smoking a pipe (second from the left of the middle row) is Freddie MacCormac of Whitchurch. This picture was taken in 1957.

Cardiff GPO Engineering Training College, Penarth in 1962. In this picture Freddie MacCormack is third from the left in the back row.

Cardiff GPO engineers seen recovering old telegraph poles in the main street of Llanbraddock, c.1956. Left to right are: John James, Don Williams, Stan Latham (foreman wearing beret) and Henry 'Boyo' De'Claire. The names of the two bystanders who got into the act are unknown!

Cardiff GPO engineers installing telephone poles for the new telephone system at Ball Road, Llanrumney. Left to right are Henry 'Boyo' De'Claire, Don Williams, Larry Gibbons, Stan Latham, and John James, c.1956.

Reginald Perring (centre) shows his safe driving medals to his fellow ambulance drivers. Jack Le Warre (left) and Harry Edwards (right). Blackweir ambulance depot.

Ambulance driver Reginald Perring fills up while Jack Le Warre looks on at Blackweir ambulance depot.

'Say Cheese!' These main fitting shop workers at the British Steel Corporation, East Moors Works, all have a smile on their faces, 1978.

AA Insurance staff members at Fanum House. Anthony Edwards (60), Lee Williams (50) Michelle Wilcox (30) and Amanda Harvey (40) celebrated their 'decade' birthdays in 2000.

This shot of a Rapides G-ALAT was taken by Mervyn Amundson. 'Three Cardif-Jersey return trips in a Rapide was a bloody hard day's work, especially in bad weather', according to Captain Kenneth G. Wakefield.

Doug Gloyn, Bob Ryan, George Bowcher, Bill Bartram and Roy Cook were all panel shop workers who were employed by Romilly Motors Coach Builders, Canton, in the 1940s.

'Tin Bashers' Viv Sanson (kneeling), Billy Charles and Dougie Gloyn (standing) working at T.S. Grimshaw, Machen Place, Canton, during the 1950s.

The Grimshaw workforce find time to pose for a photograph, *c.*1950.

Belinda Dymott, aged 17, was the only girl in a class of 22 studying for her City and Guild 1st Vehicle Certificate in 1990.

In the bottom right hand corner can be seen Chivers malt and vinegar factory. The building with the smoke coming from it is the original Ely Brewery, *c*.1940.

Ely Lodge Hospital staff, August 1933.

These pupil midwives from Queen's Maternity Hospital, St Andrew's Crescent, pictured in November 1949, were on call at any time during the day or night.

Members of the Cardiff Corporation Tramway Rolling Stock Department, 31 October 1932.

Bill Boyce and John Meazey, telegraph messengers at the main post office in Westgate Street, 1940.

The 280ft-long cooling bed of the bar mill at the Castle Works of Guest Keen & Nettlefolds (South Wales Limited), c.1967.

<#>

When East Moors Steelworks closed in 1978 some 3,000 workers had to find new jobs.

Law Court Magistrates staff posed on the steps of the Crown Court for this picture, *c.*1988.

Sir William Reardon Smith, the ship owner and philanthropist, can be seen seated in centre of this picture, *c*.1920.

Horse buses first appeared on the streets of Cardiff in 1845 and were followed by horse trams in 1872. The one in this rare picture is travelling down Corporation Road in Grangetown.

This truly remarkable picture was taken, like the one at the bottom of the previous page, by Alfred Freke who had a studio in Duke Street. It shows Watson's Saw Mills, East Canal Wharf, in around 1885.

Western Mail stereo department overseer Viv Noel is seated on a chair presented to him by his workmates on the occasion of his retirement. Left to right: Ken Miles, John Baldwin, Brian Lee, Arthur Parry, John Sweeney, Jimmy Stevens, Bob Potter, John Haines, Len Johnson, Bert Bradshaw, Stan Chamberlain, David Thomas (managing director) and Harry Ware.

Another retirement at Thomson House. This time it's the turn of Silias Wilson, overseer of the *South Wales Echo* stereo department, and he appears to be very happy that he's leaving! His workmates include Bob Potter, Eric Stoker, Bernard Roles, Peter Norris, John Sweeney, Reg Potter, Ronnie Bibbings, John English, Len Johnson, Brian Lee and Ken Miles, *c.*1980.

Lord Kenneth Thomson (extreme right) chatting to stereotypers John English, Stan Parsons, Bernard Roles and Brian Lee at the *Western Mail & Echo* building in Park Street. The building is the current home of the newspapers and was opened by his father, Roy Thomson, on 20 June 1961.

Harry Ferris, who worked for the *Western Mail & Echo* for more than half-a-century and who retired in 1979, is seen working in the process room at the old *Echo* offices in St Mary Street, *c.*1938.

One of Cardiff's many Land Army girls was Phyllis Condon, née Latham, who worked for the Forestry Commission at the outskirts of the city during World War Two. This photograph was taken in January 1942.

Cardiff Home Guard, *c.*1940. Third from the left standing is Bill Smith who was wounded at Gallipoli during World War One. He worked as a park keeper for 35 years.

City of Cardiff bus drivers have been safely transporting Cardiffians throughout the city for many years. But, as the picture below shows, accidents can happen.

This picture was taken in 1985, at the retirement of bus driver Ivor Beaven (left) with Mr Yeates, manager of Cardiff Bus. After starting work as a conductor, Mr Beaven went on to drive every type of bus from trolley to single-deckers.

Maintenance staff at the old Roath Bus Depot posed for this picture before the closure of the depot, c.1983.

Ivor Beaven seen driving the last trolley bus to the Pier Head. Trolley buses stopped running in 1969, but a special planned farewell ride to the Docks took place in early January 1970.

This was the trolley bus terminus for Gabalfa at the top end of Whitchurch Road, c.1968.

Littlewoods office manager John Cargill holds the tape for Miss Backhouse, the manageress, to cut at the official opening of Littlewoods extension in Charles Street, 1970. The store closed in 1998.

New Theatre staff group photograph, c.1980.

Lipton's, the grocers, had branches at St John's Square, The Hayes, Albany Road, Carlisle Street, Clifton Street, Whitchurch Road and Woodville Road.

SPORTING MOMENTS

The Welsh team parading before the Duke of Edinburgh at the 1958 Empire and Commonwealth Games held at Cardiff Arms Park.

The Games marathon runners having left the stadium are seen passing the now demolished Cambrian Buildings in Newport Road. They still had 24 miles to go!

Australia's Dave Power is well clear at the 15-mile mark.

Just three miles to run and Dave Power gets a cheer and a clap from these garage workers. He eventually won in a time of 2hrs, 22 mins, 45.6 secs, establishing a new Games record.

Pam John, née Dalton, (Roath Cardiff Harriers) who has the unique distinction of having run for Wales on the track and cross-country in the 1970s as well as winning a team bronze at bowls at the 2000 Commonwealth Games.

'On Your Marks!' A field of eight international women athletes line up at the start of the 880 yards event at the Welsh Games, Maindy Stadium. Pam John is wearing No.9. Note the packed stands which have now been demolished. Only the cycle track remains.

Above shows Ted Williams (Cardiff 100 Miles Club) attempting a roller racing record at Sophia Gardens in the 1950s. After retiring from the cycling circuit, he became a showjumping competitor and is seen below competing at the St Mellon's Show in 1969.

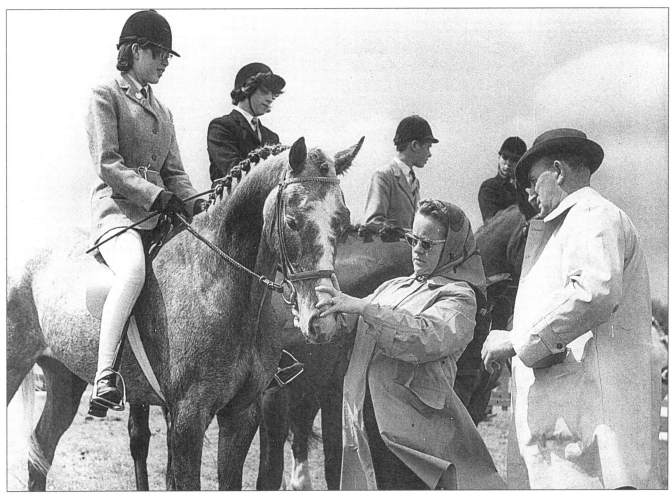

Olive and Trevor Jenks, from Rumney, judging the riding pony class at the Peterstone Horse Show, 1970.

The famed Reg Harris (second right) is seen here racing at Maindy Stadium in 1951. Leading is Cyril Bardsley and fourth right is Ted Williams.

Wales's greatest walker, Steve Barry of Cardiff, wearing No.31, broke many Welsh and British records. He won a gold medal in the 30km walk at the 1982 Commonwealth Games in Brisbane, beating a world-class field.

Dai Barry, wearing No.73, father of Steve Barry, was Wales's most successful walker in the 1950s, winning nine Welsh championship titles.

Eddie Lee took up athletics rather late in life and became one of Wales's best-ever veteran marathon runners.

The start of the 1939 International Cross-Country Championships at Ely Racecourse. Wearing No.22 right of picture is the great Welsh marathon runner Tom Richards.

The Ex-Internationals football team who played mostly for charity. Back row (left to right): Glyn Potter (manager), Lew Clayton, Ron Stitfall, Graham Vearncombe, Roy Saunders, Colin Baker, Percy Davies (trainer). Front row: Jimmy Scoular, Terry Medwin, Mel Charles, John Charles, Ivor Allchurch, Brian Edgley.

A huge crowd turned up for the Cardiff City v Arsenal game at Ninian Park in 1968. The player who has signed his name on the photograph (second left of picture) is none other than Cardiff's own John Toshack.

These two pictures of Roath Rangers AC were taken at Roath Park Recreation Grounds in the 1950s.

This picture of the Cardiff Boys baseball team was taken at the Cardiff Arms Park in 1953. The gentleman seated in the centre is Tom O'Reilly, sports teacher at St Peter's Roman Catholic School. The gentleman standing extreme left wearing a blazer is Don Frost, the referee.

Paddy Hennessy shows the Lord Mayor, J.C. Edwards, how to hold a baseball bat. Others in the picture are 'Slogger' Slocombe, Alan Patton, Tommy Clarke, Johnny Bowler, Ray Knight, Trevor Rees, Bernard Leho, Arthur Wozencroft, Bill Smith, Maurice Jones, Kenny Horton and Terry Cleverly.

Charity baseball match, *c.*1960. Wearing a cap is Frank Hennessy of BBC Radio Wales. Others in the picture are Cardiff City soccer player Phil Dwyer (second right), John Tyler, Dave Burns, Richie Morgan, Ted Peterson, Paddy Hennessy, Terry 'Slogger' Slocombe, Graham Pymble, and Dai Percy.

Howells Garage baseball team, *c.*1964.

Cardiff and District RFC. The top picture was taken in 1966 and the bottom one a few years earlier.

One of Welsh rugby's all-time greats. Gareth Edwards in action for Wales against Argentina in 1976. With Barry John he formed a dazzling partnership for Cardiff, Wales and the British Lions.

Gerald Davies, a legend on the right wing for Cardiff and Wales, sweeps in for his second try of the match against Ireland at the Cardiff Arms Park in 1971.

A great son of Cardiff. Terry Holmes, scrum half extraordinary, on the attack against the Barbarians in 1985. He scored 142 tries for Cardiff.

Mark Ring, a man of many magic moments and especially a master of the wide pass. Here he lines up a kick on one of his 32 appearances for Wales.

J.P.R. Williams, generally acknowledged the most exciting full-back to play for Wales. Born in Cardiff, he played mainly for London Welsh. He won the Junior Wimbledon tennis championship in 1966. Here he leads Wales out against England in 1979.

Barry John, King of the Lions in New Zealand in 1971, launches John Dawes and John Bevan into an attack against Ireland at Cardiff Arms Park in 1971, during a golden era of Welsh rugby success.

Cardiff City Police cricket team, *c.*1933.

These Cardiff cricketers took part in a charity match at Maindy Barracks fields, now the site of Companies House, in 1949.

Reunion time. Glamorgan stalwarts gather. Left to right: Phil Clift, Allan Watkins, Wilf Wooller, Norman Hever, Haydn Davies and Jim Pleass. Wilf Wooller, who captained Wales at rugby and Glamorgan at cricket, was a sporting legend.

Barbados-born Tony Cordle arrived in Cardiff to play for the Cardiff club and then Glamorgan, for whom he became a particular favourite with the fans. Here he wears his self-made protective headgear while fielding against Middlesex in 1971. Peter Parfitt is the batsman.

Cardiff-born Gwyn Hughes on his way to a memorable 92 against the Australians at the Arms Park in 1964. He won a cricket Blue at Cambridge University and played for Cardiff and St Fagan's.

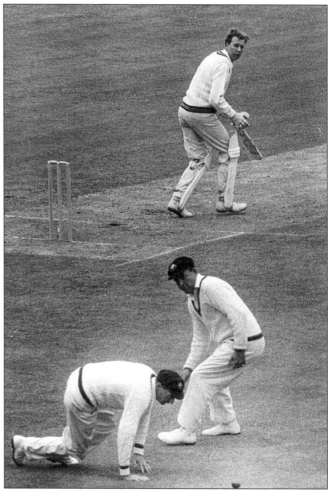

Opening the Glamorgan innings against Hampshire at Sophia Gardens in 1989 is left-hander Hugh Morris, who scored 18,520 first-class runs between 1981 and 1997 at an average of 41.06. His highest score was an unbeaten 233 against Warwickshire in Cardiff in 1997.

Roath (Cardiff) Harriers cross-country team at Maindy Stadium, *c*.1963. Back row (left to right): Bob Tawton (official), Dave Bessant, John 'Buster' Jones, Cecil Oakley, Bernard Gallivan, Norman Horrell, John Burrows, unknown, Brian Griffiths, Haydon Tawton, Alf Jenson, Ken Harris (official), unknown, Bernard Tucker, unknown. Front row: Walter Sutherland, Dougie Mends, unknown, Mac Beames, Tony Callagahan, Dougie Lane, Peter Mason.

Sixth from the left back row is Welsh AAA national coach Jim Alford, of Cardiff, who won the Empire Games mile gold medal at Sydney in 1938. Bonny Jones, Haydon Tawton, Dai Pritchard, Tony Clemo and Dougie Lane are some of the others in the picture taken at Lilleshall in 1959.

In 1964 Roath (Cardiff) Harrier Brian Lee receives a New Year's (Nos Galan) message from the Lord Mayor Alderman, W.J. Hartland, to the Chairman of the Mountain Ash Urban District Council, before running the 20 miles to Mountain Ash to deliver it.

Eighteen years later and Brian Lee (Les Croupiers Cardiff) is seen winning the 1982 Dow Corning Barry Half-Marathon Over-45s race in a time of exactly 1hr 20 mins.

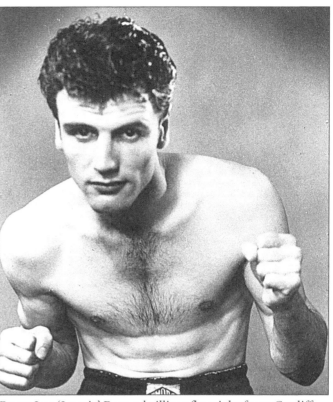

Splott-born Welsh and British featherweight champion boxer Gordon Blakey won 26 of his 33 professional fights in the 1960s.

Boxer Len 'Luggie' Rees, a brilliant flyweight from Cardiff.

St Mary's Canton AFC, 1958.

Rhydypenau Junior School football team, 1954. The lad with the baggy shorts extreme right is Dougie Lane.

Dougie Lane (left) asks the 1958 British Commonwealth Games 100 yards champion Keith Gardener of Jamaica for his autograph. The Westgate Street flats can be seen in the back ground.

The same Dougie Lane as above, a few years later, leading Tony Clemo (left) and Paul Darney (right) in a club cross-country race at Gabalfa.

Rhydypenau Junior School baseball team were winners of the Cosslet Cup in 1954. Seated on the bench second left is Dougie Lane.

Roath Park soccer team, 1956–7.

Ten-a-side rugby Welsh national finalists St Mary's School, who represented Cardiff in 1996. Back row (left to right): Steve Lloyd (parent), Nathan Powell, Lawrence Selio, Carwyn Lloyd, Richard Clements, Ross O'Donnell, Andrew Davies (teacher). Front row: Andrew Niblett, David Allen, Gavin Davies (captain), Max Kelly, Paul Collins, Luke Hopkins. Brewery Field, Bridgend.

St Mary's School netball team, 1989. The three girls in the back row are (left to right) Katherine Kelleher, Natalie Dooley and Fiona Kimberly. Others in the picture include Joanna Cross, Charlotte Smith, Emily Nash, Victoria Williams, Susanna Crowe, Louise Humphries and Lucy Burns.

St Mary's RC Primary School netball team, 1990. The teachers are Mrs O'Reilly and Mr Gorman.

St Mary's RC School junior rugby team, 1989.

CAPITOL THEATRE

The much-loved Capitol Theatre which opened in 1921 and was demolished in 1978 to make way for the Capitol Exchange Shopping Centre which was opened in 1991. The pictures in this chapter are all taken from the Capitol Theatre album for November 1937–January 1940. The film *Bluebeard's Eighth Wife*, starring Claudette Colbert and Gary Cooper, was playing at the theatre when this picture was taken in 1938.

The Capitol Theatre orchestra, 1939.

Frank Davison, the resident organist at his Lafleur Theatre Organ.

Christmas 1938 and members of the orchestra help with the stirring of the Christmas pudding. No doubt they are playing something seasonal.

A delivery lorry backs into the Capitol in February 1939.

The great Welsh politician David Lloyd George (1863–1945) visited the theatre on St David's Day, 1938.

Her Majesty Queen Mary's visit on 6 April 1938. She attended a charity matinee in aid of nursing associations. The highlight of the show was said to be when the Treorchy Male Voice Choir, who came straight from the coalmine in their working clothes, sang to her.

The famed Hancock Brewery greys are on their way to Nazareth House with a Christmas tree for the children.

Gene Autry, the 'Singing Cowboy', visited Cardiff in 1938 and hundreds of his fans turned out to see him. He made his first film in 1934 and his last in 1976. He is seen here walking towards the Capitol Theatre.

.